PREPARING FOR COLLEGE THEATRE:

A Guide For Performers, Technicians, and Designers

For Students :: By Students

Constructed by Roman Sanchez

Roman Sanchez

2020

First Printing: 2020
ISBN 978-0-578-67062-1
Roman D. Sanchez
www.limeartsproductions.org

Ordering Information:
Special discounts are available on quantity purchases by corporations, associations, educators and others. For details, contact the author at the above listed address.
U.S. trade bookstores and wholesalers: Please contact Roman Sanchez, email: romansanchezcompany@gmail.com.

TABLE OF CONTENTS

FOREWORD

Here is what I love about this book, PREPARING FOR COLLEGE THEATRE, that Roman has so generously put together.

I love that it is truly for students from the perspective of someone who was recently a student, someone who has just traveled this landscape, and has a fresh, contemporary take on the experiences they had in the process and how it informed their life.

I love that it explicitly states that one size, one experience, one way, what everyone tells you, simply does not fit all. You have choices.

I love that the encouragement is for each to make their own path, but with some real guideposts to explore along the way. It is a frequently quoted statement, but I find it even more true now than ever, Lao-Tzu in the Tao Te Ching wrote, "the journey of a thousand miles begins with a single step." This book powerfully encourages you to take that step.

And then…. I love that this book encourages "adaptation." You aren't stuck. You have the capacity to change direction if you find yourself on a path that is not leading you where you want to go. The encouragement in this book is to develop that adaptive muscle that is so critical on any journey.

I love that this book is both pragmatic and inspirational. This book flat out lists everything from terms you need to know and where to go to know more. That sense of ongoing investigation, invention, curiosity, are essential tools on this journey.

And I love that this book encourages "practice." The Greek root of "practice" is the word "praxis," which means the balance of action and reflection. This book encourages that balance, but really speaks to the fact that you need to "do" to "know."

Thank you Roman for not waiting to write this and get it out into the world. It is important and necessary now, in this time. It really does speak to this point in the lives of the world and the generations to come. When so much is uncertain and unknowable, this book gives rich and viable sources of options that can help us all navigate forward.

Michael Fields
Director, California State Summer School for the Arts
Producing Artistic Director, Dell'Arte International School of Physical Theatre

INTRODUCTION

Prior to your entrance into the world of higher education, you most likely haven't been allowed to think for yourself. The educational system has most likely failed you by teaching you to memorize irrelevant facts rather than employing the critical-thinking skills found in the process of learning. You're just starting to figure out who you are—molded by the community that you were raised in, your teachers, and your peers. You've endured petty dress codes, SAT scores, cliques, homecomings, bad yearbook photos, and all the other glorious highs and devastating lows that come with the years before entering college. And now, you're asked to make a single decision and commitment that will likely impact the rest of your life. No pressure.

I was in your place not too long ago. I started as a child performer, taking acting and dance classes, but I lived in a small rural town in California. I did not have the experience or the tools to make an informed decision, nor did I know where to find the resources to help me make this decision. My teacher helped the best he could, I researched online and read books. Fortunately, I got the most help from a summer intensive I was accepted into, led by the person who wrote the foreword to this book.

I have now navigated my way through college theatre, and the theatre world at large, by taking many paths. I started as a performer, fell in love with directing, started enjoying the behind-the-scenes work as a stage manager, became a production manager, and now I identify myself as "a producer, director and educator." It took me 18 years to come to this—and I would not be surprised if I shifted my career again in the future.

In short, there is no one answer that is right or applicable to everyone. Too many circumstances stand in the way and we all want something specific out of higher education. No single mentor, educator or theatre practitioner holds the answers for everyone. Neither do I.

To that end, I have called on the help of several hundred theatre practitioners from Alaska to Florida and Maine to Hawaii. These are folks who are recent graduates or were currently studying a form of theatre at a higher education level. There is a rich diversity in this pool of interviewees—locations, majors, aspirations, experience, etc.—and though diverse in scope, many experiences had common themes and focuses. These findings helped me to articulate and challenged my preconceived thoughts on theatre's higher education system. Hereafter, we will refer to all theatre training programs (two-year colleges, four-year colleges and universities, trade schools and conservatories) as "colleges."

In the spirit of my mission to include as many firsthand pieces of advice, stories and perspectives, you'll find some of my friends and colleagues' quotes. I hope the variety of experiences showcase the many routes available to you and can give you a number of things to consider.

On behalf of all of us, welcome! Thank you for choosing this path, taking the risk and continuing where we've left off. This process is daunting, uncertain and demanding. I know the information in this book will help lighten the load.

Roman Sanchez, 2020

PERKS OF AN ARTS EDUCATION IN THE CREATIVE ECONOMY

An arts education has many definitions—each dependent on the individual. Like any schooling, you get out what you put in.

"What is the value of an arts education?"
If you're reading this book, I probably don't have to explain this.

What I would like to mention, however, is the resources and data Americans for the Arts releases frequently. In 2019, they published a plethora of new data to help governing bodies fully comprehend the value the arts have financially, morally and medically.

Their data shows that numbers are clearly in favor of the arts—it's proven. The arts, culture, and entertainment sectors have employed more individuals around the world each year. These creative industries started partnering with STEM careers to help with imagination and innovation.

But what does this mean for individual artists trying to make a career in their respective industries? Is there actual money circulating in the arts? Is it possible to have a steady and fulfilling, but most of all financially stable career in the arts? Well, I don't know. Of the hundreds of artists I've had the privilege of meeting and collaborating with, there's only one thing in common: It's all circumstantial.

I can't tell you whether or not you'll have a steady job for the rest of your life or if you'll have a solid retirement plan or if you'll be happy creating art for the next 70 years. But I can tell you that the arts undoubtedly serve many purposes on the local, state and federal level and one of those reasons is serving as a catalyst in the economy. Thus, an education in the arts provides countless opportunities for success beyond the stereotypical "successful actor" mold.

No matter what path your career takes you, an arts education will give you the five most marketable and most-needed skills in life:

Adaptability
Communication
Collaboration
Creativity
Time Management

SUMMER PROGRAMS

Aside from the typical high school theatre experience, classes and after-school productions, serious theatre students should consider finding other opportunities to explore learning their craft in a new setting. Summer programs can be a great way to experience:

1. The environment of a college setting
2. Working with professionals
3. Exploring what college or career path is right for you
4. A cohort of like-minded artists

Many people recognize the importance of a summer theatre experience as it is here that students often realize whether or not they want to pursue an education in the arts and what kind of program might best fit their needs. Of course, summer programs help create lifelong friends and start networking opportunities with your cohort that will come in handy in the future workforce.

These summer programs are provided by state or local agencies, regional or community theatres and by various colleges or theatre programs. Some things to keep an eye out for when thinking about which summer programs to apply for are the same criteria we discuss later in this book when looking for a college program:

- Faculty
- Curriculum
- Location
- Class Size
- Reputation /Alumni
- Cost

One more applicable criterion is whether college credit is available. If the main reason you're interested in a summer program is to test whether or not a specific style or training works for you, I'd recommend searching for a program that looks similar to what you're seeking.

For example, if you're interested in conservatory-style training, try to find a summer intensive that packs your schedule with classes similar to that of a conservatory. If you're contemplating whether or not you're capable of living far away from your family by yourself in a college dorm, try to find a program held on a university campus that houses you in its dorms and perhaps spans more than a couple weeks. If you want hands-on design or technical experience, look for "maker" programs that allow you to work in shops, construct things or let you explore the design process.

One positive impact you'll find in any program is that you'll be surrounded by like-minded individuals. Each person's path led them to the point where they are in a summer program because they are interested in or have a passion for theatre. Take full advantage of what will be a never-ending process of networking—these are practitioners who you'll run into throughout your career.

Everyone I've spoken to who attended a summer program has stayed in contact with some of their peers and some relationships have grown throughout the years—starting businesses, creating work, attending the same school and so on. This takeaway is invaluable.

"I went to Ithaca College's summer program and it was really great. It gave me the feel of college life and the logistics of being a theatre major. I also did a two-week program at the American Academy of Dramatic Arts, which was equally great. It showed me the intensity of conservatory style training, which helped me realize it was something I didn't want. But all of these programs gave me the opportunity to explore theatre as a career (and not just a hobby) in a more intense setting while still under the safety blanket of education. Logistically, they just exposed me to more plays, names, and terminology."
Hannah Cohen, New York University

"I went to the California State Summer School for the Arts between my sophomore and junior years of high school. It was maybe the most transformational month of my life. I grew into myself. I was able to find my independent artistic voice and focus on exactly what I wanted to

accomplish. It was after CSSSA that I decided I wanted to pursue a
B.F.A. in Acting in college."

Carson Harvey, SUNY Purchase

"I attended the Northwestern Summer High School Institute,
nicknamed 'Cherubs,' the summer before my senior year of high
school. The program was a really immersive and magical exploration
of all aspects of theater, and helped me clarify that I wanted to pursue
the arts in college."

Justine Marler, University of North Carolina School of the Arts

COLLEGE TYPES

There are many "types" of higher education training programs and each is designed for different types of learners and artists.

Options include:

- Two-Year Colleges & Certificate Programs
- Liberal Arts Colleges & Universities
- Conservatories
- Conservatories on Liberal Arts Campuses
- Trade Schools

Two-year colleges are a great place to gain valuable, practical experience in various aspects of theatre. Two-year colleges will allow you to: seek an Associate of Arts (A.A.) degree to transfer to a four-year school, to enter a focus program that offers a two-year certificate, and/or to enroll in theatre classes and work on productions for the experience. Whatever path you choose, the experiences you will receive at a two-year college can be a springboard toward a career in the arts. In particular, the two-year technical theatre programs can prepare students for an immediate career backstage.

Liberal arts colleges and universities by definition complete coursework in a wide variety of other areas of study—the humanities, sciences, creative arts, social sciences and so on. This translates into a list of general education (G.E.) classes where each state and system has different requirements. It is in this type of training program that students will take approximately 35% of the units in their major's classes and 65% of the units in liberal arts classes (i.e. math, biology, history, English, foreign language, etc.). Some students and practitioners look at this as an opportunity to become a well-rounded artist, a chance to expand your knowledge beyond your craft and an opportunity to apply your creativity into other topics. These institutions also allow room for double-majors and minors (more information on these later) and take approximately four years to complete, often in the form of a Bachelor of Arts (B.A.) degree.

Performance-based conservatories allow for approximately 75-90% of the units in the major's classes and the rest of the units in classes that aren't directly related to the major, but still are considered applicable. For example, at CalArts, electives range from A Brief History of Ventriloquism to Theatrical Unions to Theatre Management. Another great example is Yale School of Drama's course plan, which contains classes ranging from Clown to Yoga. All of this is to say that a majority of the courses within the curriculum are tailored in a way to create intensive training for their students. Performance-based conservatories range from one to three years for a certificate program and longer for a Bachelor of Fine Arts (B.F.A) degree.

Some conservatories are located on the campuses of Liberal Arts Universities—these are a special niche. Examples of these include The Actors Studio at Pace University, Trinity Repertory Company at Brown University and The Conservatory of Theatre Arts at Webster University. These are conservatory-style programs held on the campus of a larger liberal arts university, providing a unique experience to be surrounded by both types of learning environments. You can typically earn either a B.A or B.F.A. from these types of programs, too.

Trade schools are a popular option for those interested in theatre technology. Examples include Rigging International Group, IATSE Training Trust and the SAE Institute. Most of these programs are for non-degree seeking students looking to dive deep into a specific niche of technical theatre (sound engineering, theatrical rigging, union safety procedures, etc.) for a limited amount of time. While some programs do offer degrees, most students usually receive certificates at the end of their training. Folks who choose this route typically are planning on going straight into the workforce after the program, using the newfound niche education to their advantage.

"I chose a large four-year research university because I wanted the option to take Anthropology and Psychology courses in addition to a conservatory program. Boston University is well known for being so large and so well-rounded. I wanted those options, while still being in such a tight-knit, socially conscious conservatory theatre program with

an emphasis on physical training. The program is structured like most B.A. programs, though it's a B.F.A."

Maggie Markham, Boston University

"I chose a two-year community college to study Entertainment Stage Technology because of the possibility of transferring to a larger university later. It also allowed for having a much more intensive curriculum without the irrelevant courses."

Kelsey N. Forero, Valencia College and North Carolina School of the Arts

"I wanted a theatrical education in a big research university. It was important for me to be surrounded by people studying all kinds of things, allowing me to have a broader perspective of the world. I also wanted to minor in Business Marketing and a Bachelor of Arts program allowed me to make that possible."

Tyler Joseph Ellis, University of Southern California

"It is important to me that my life is surrounded by diverse backgrounds and subjects to enrich my empathetic relationship to the world. I chose a four-year liberal arts degree [for undergrad] because it offered a well-rounded education in multiple fields. Being a well-rounded person can only enhance my understanding of different ways of life. Theatre and life are one and the same to me so engaging in different ideas makes the work more fulfilling and the work more relatable to audiences."

Shea King, Humboldt State University and University of Idaho

"Conservatory—I wanted to have a more strict and structured curriculum when it came to training as an actor. I knew a conservatory environment would challenge me artistically first and academically second. That layout/order only aids me in the classroom. I also knew this structure would allow me to fulfill all three of my passions: acting, dancing and singing."

CamRon Stewart, University of North Carolina School of the Arts

"I wanted the full 'college experience'. I have an interest in becoming a teacher some day and knew I will need at least a bachelor's degree to

19

teach high school but I also knew that a two-year program wouldn't feel like enough for me. I didn't have any professional training before AMDA so I felt I needed a four-year program."

Jennifer Horne, The American Musical and Dramatic Academy

COLLEGE AREA OF STUDY (MAJOR)

By this point, whether or not you have completed a summer program that has confirmed your aspirations to further your theatrical education, you still have many factors to consider.

Some of the more practical factors deal with logistics: tuition and scholarships, geographic location, and family support. Others pertain to preference: curriculum, class sizes, faculty and reputation. We'll visit each of these variables later but let's start with what area you'd like to study.

Many theatre practitioners want to do it all: direct, act, write, design, produce. While most can agree that it is important to know all theatre workers' jobs and processes, very few majors/programs allow for you to deeply study more than one area. The ones that do offer a broad spectrum of theatre courses will often categorize this area of study as "General Theatre" or "Theatre Arts" but a closer look at the curriculum will confirm what specifically you'll be learning.

The most important thing is that you should choose a major or emphasis that will make you happy for years to come. If you do end up in a program that is narrow in scope, you still can learn about other areas of theatre by:

1. Making friends who are studying in other areas
2. Finding artists who are practicing professionals near your school
3. Asking your department head or adviser if you can shadow a shop manager for a couple hours or for the duration of a show (some state universities offer work study opportunities in costume and scenic shops—an opportunity to learn hard skill sets and have a part-time job)
4. Serve as a crew member, builder or technician for as many of your program's productions as possible

5. Keeping an eye out for student productions or community theatre opportunities—these are low-risk learning opportunities that get you hands-on experience
6. Creating your own program of study—an opportunity available at a plethora of programs

Choosing your major is an important decision, but most colleges give you some time to think about it, often schools do not even let you decide until your sophomore year. That said, be wary of the programs that don't let you take theatre courses until your sophomore or junior years because how else will you get experience to make an informed decision if you aren't allowed to take the classes. Whatever you decide, make sure that your major nourishes you, makes you happy and that you are passionate about your choice.

"I switched to the Theatre Department after discovering Stage Management by chance. The Design & Production degree was the best/closest fit to Stage Management and also allowed more flexibility in courses (substituting independent studies in for other classes). It also encouraged a holistic approach where I would interact with all aspects of the design and production process of a show."
Miranda Erin Campbell, Purdue University

"I've known for a very long time I wanted to be in education in some capacity. I chose the Theatre Education major because it connected my two favorite things: theatre and teaching. I want to make theatre magic with high schoolers and this program sets me up to do just that."
Madison Comeaux, Central Washington University

"I chose to major in Acting because of the insurmountable joy I find in learning about the craft. Being on stage or on screen is a gift and an honor and the opportunity to study acting, voice and physical techniques that would enhance my skill sets is immeasurable. The byproducts of learning this craft appealed to me too—knowing that communication, empathy, and leadership can be applied to just about any industry. All of this to say, the opportunity to immerse oneself in acting is a privilege and I'm grateful to have had the chance to do so."
Melissa Schwarz, CSU Northridge

"I found myself pursuing a B.F.A. with the writing and literature department, which was wonderful and served me well, and all my free time was spent helping the theatre department. I particularly enjoy seeing the big picture and helping individuals shine for themselves which is why directing seemed to suit me best in graduate school. Plus, my literary background has enabled me to have great script analysis skills which also helps the role of the director."
 Kaitlyn Samuel Rosin, University of Evansville and Actors Studio
Drama School

COLLEGE MINOR

If you find yourself at a higher education institution that provides the option to have a minor, you might consider it.

Simply put, a minor is a second area of study. Sometimes they complement the major (like a dance minor for a musical theatre major) and sometimes they're completely unrelated (like a soils minor for a playwriting major).

Some minors that practitioners have noted as helping them in their theatre careers include: art, business, dance, English, entrepreneurship, film, foreign languages, math, music and psychology. Some programs allow you to double-focus on two areas of theatre, too. Examples include performance and technical theatre tracks, or management and theatre design and technology. You may want to look at schools that allow these opportunities if you are equally interested in two areas of study.

The non-theatre minors also provide the opportunity to learn a subject that could be used down the road as a backup plan or day job. Minors are typically only found at liberal arts institutions. To minor in a subject means you may be adding time to your educational experience—sometimes a semester or a year, depending on the subject.

Now, if you still aren't positive if you want to pursue theatre as a career or want theatre to be a backup plan, this is also valid. Some practitioners who share similar sentiments have elected to minor in their respective theatre area. This would allow for a student to still study some theatre while studying another subject more comprehensively. Remember, though, the outlook for jobs in performing arts is increasingly bright as the world becomes more and more dependent on technology and entertainment.

"I chose a drama minor because I knew theatre was my passion and the minor still gave me tools to turn theatre from a hobby into a career."

Meghann Heinrich, Walla Walla University

"I'm glad I chose to minor in Theatre because I wound up not liking my Zoology major and switching it to Theatre. Without starting as a minor, I would not have known my true calling."

Epigmenio Villareal, Taylor University

"Theater, in addition to being my career path, was an easy umbrella major under which to take a broad range of coursework, and which allowed me the time and freedom to do minors in two other departments."

Lynne Marie Rosenberg, Vassar College

FACULTY

Much like your peers, you'll be around your faculty for several years. The faculty of a theatre department can weigh heavily in your choice of schools. Here are some characteristics and qualities of a good faculty member that could be important in your search:

1. Excellent Communication Skills
2. Motivational Ability
3. Accessibility to Students
4. Theoretical vs Professional Practitioner
5. Currently Practicing vs Retired Practitioner
6. Quality, breadth, and extent of their resume or experience
7. Crafts their curriculum as a response to their students' needs and experiences
8. Connection to potential employers

It is critical for faculty members to be able to communicate clearly with their students. Looking at various faculty members' syllabi prior to enrolling at a school is a smart way to determine how teachers structure their classes, gives insight to their communication style, and shows if they are current in their practices. Share these syllabi with your high school theatre teacher to get their feedback.

It is also important to sit in on classes (either in person or electronically) to view your potential mentor's motivational ability, hear their communication style and get a sense of their personality. Personality, and how teachers connect with their students is critical since you will be potentially working with this person for the next several years. Additionally, their accessibility via office hours and other times throughout the day are important when needing clarifications on assignments or to further discuss lectures.

Some of the most well-known and well-regarded departments have a shared quality in their instructors—they're active practitioners and good educators. This means while they are part- or full-time faculty members, they also continue to professionally practice their craft and their ability to teach. Some weigh these aspects highly. While these faculty are still practicing "in the industry," they are continuously immersed in the evolving trends and movements, which a good teacher can translate into the classroom.

Another common quality in faculty are those who did not practice their craft professionally, thus their pedagogy is primarily theoretical. This isn't always a bad thing, in particular theatre historians, theatre literature teachers and some dramaturgs do not have as much practical experience, but can be highly respected for their ability to frame discussions, compare literary texts and provide vivid lectures on trends throughout theatre history. Remember, again, that when you are looking for an artistic home to go and study that you can trust the faculty members, be inspired by them and will want to show up to your classes each day.

The final question to ask is: Can your faculty help you get jobs when you are done training with them?

"I chose ACT because of the faculty there at the time I applied—Jeffery Crockett was head of voice and Stephen Buescher was head of movement. The two of them were two of the most brilliant minds I've ever encountered and to work with them was a blessing."
Belle Aykroyd, American Conservatory Theater

"I am learning from people who are still designing shows and have the opportunity to work with some of the most well-known theatre and opera companies in the midwest."
Hannah Muren, The Conservatory of Theatre Arts at Webster University

"Our professors are people who are working actors, so it's really cool to know that the lectures that we were getting were fresh and new."
Antonio Romero Jr., The University of Texas at El Paso

COURSE CURRICULUM

Curriculum can play a factor in decision-making, too.

Course catalogues are made by school administrators and faculty that outline the courses offered by each department. Most departments have this available on their official website for perusal. Some students have specific things they're looking for in their curriculum (for example, wanting lots of classes in movement or acting techniques or not wanting lighting design classes) and this can be a great resource.

Course load by semester is something else to note. Some intensive programs are built in a way that have their students in classes 30-40 hours a week. Asking a theatre adviser about course load per semester or trimester is a good way to guesstimate how much time you'll spend outside of classes. This time can be spent studying, rehearsing for shows, working part-time, getting an internship, etc.

Other curriculum-related questions to ask:

1. At what year are students allowed to participate or audition in departmental productions?
2. Do undergraduate students get to design in main stage productions?
3. Are hands-on practicums or electives available?
4. How frequently are guest instructors hosted?
5. Do graduate students assist or teach undergraduate courses?
6. If I am a performance-track student, can I also take classes in other theatre areas?
7. Do I get credit for being involved in a main stage production?
8. Are substitutions allowed for various courses?
9. If I was to wait and transfer in, what classes would count?
10. Is there flexibility in completing your curriculum in a shorter amount of time?

"The curriculum is rigorous, especially in your first year. You take a full academic load while also having a full-time or part-time job. There are multiple classes for a single subject. For example, a beginning and advanced marketing class, as well as multiple financial classes. There's more robust learning as the curriculum builds over your training. Yale also has an emphasis on teaching with case studies so you're learning from real situations that theaters have encountered."

Caitlin Volz, Chapman University and Yale School of Drama

"I chose this program because I wanted the freedom and encouragement to pursue performance as well as technical opportunities. The ability to explore different areas within theatre: stage management, lighting design, dramaturgy—classes that have broadened by knowledge as a theatre-maker."

Caitlin McFann, San Francisco State University

LOCATION

Another noteworthy factor: location, location, location. Location can be closely compared alongside the factor of reputation/alumni.

One of the great things about The Juilliard School is that it is located in the heart of New York City, one of the hubs for aspiring actors and talented techies. Some will want to study in a completely opposite environment—a rural or suburban setting—like The University of the South's town of Sewanee, Tennessee, population 2,300. Always know that you don't need to study in New York or Los Angeles to have a theatrical career there. Also know that there are boisterously booming theatre scenes around regional theatres everywhere in the country, with lots of job and gig opportunities. Some of these noteworthy regions include: Boston, Chicago, San Francisco, Seattle, Minneapolis, Atlanta, Miami and Washington, D.C.

Another component of location is how far away your school is from your home. Some people want or need to live as close to home as possible—whether it's the financial constraints of out-of-state tuition or the likelihood of homesickness.

Further attributes that may be of interest when looking at locations include:
- Are there any community or regional theatres nearby?
- Are there ample part-time job opportunities around town or on campus?
- What do the program's theatres and rehearsal spaces look like?
- Does the aesthetic of the town or city appeal to you?
- Do you feel safe in this town or city?
- What kind of housing opportunities exist?

"Location influenced me because in-state tuition is cheaper, gas isn't a major expense because I live so close and I was already familiar with the surrounding area."
Martin William Cicco Jr., University of South Alabama

"Due to Linfield's location, I was able to commute to Portland and receive real work experience. It allowed me to exercise what I was learning and see the effect in real-time while still growing and preparing myself for the professional world."

Antoine Johnson, Linfield University

"I've landed a handful of gigs in the community theatre scene. The community's reputation—and especially the theatre community's— is stellar. It is small but mighty. Instead of walking into the area feeling a heaping amount of competition, I walked in and made a family."

Kiara Hudlin, Humboldt State University

CLASS SIZE

Class size is another factor to consider.

If you are at a liberal arts institution, chances are the class size of your general education classes (especially lectures) will be significantly larger than your major classes. If you're a learner who needs one-on-one attention from educators, this might be a red flag. However, some institutions have smaller class sizes for freshmen, or they provide "cohorts," which are teams of students that take a few of their gen eds together. Many schools are trying to combat larger class sizes with innovative approaches with regards to first-year students.

Some questions to consider:

1. Does the institution offer smaller lecture class options?
2. Does the institution offer online or hybrid classes?
3. If at a conservatory, what is the enrollment cap of each incoming class?
4. Can you imagine yourself training alongside that many people for several years?

You can get answers to these questions by asking your adviser and other faculty. Also, remember to find students at that institution and ask them the same questions—the true answer probably is somewhere in the middle of their responses.

"It was a small school with small class sizes in a wide variety of topics. My professors knew my name, I knew all my classmates. The town embraced the students, instead of seeing them as a nuisance."
Heather E. Cribbs, Flagler College

"I wanted an educational setting that would allow me to get personalized attention from my professors. I know that I operate much better as a big fish in a little pond. Plus, about 50% of theater isn't what you know, it's who you know. I knew I'd have a better chance

connecting with my professors and peers if I was going to a smaller college. So I looked for something small."

Hunter Anderson, Hastings College

"L.C.C.C. has a smaller class size, average of 15 students per class, and because of this I felt that I got the attention that I truly needed from my instructors and advisers. Because of our small size, we were allowed a much larger section of creative freedom and formed a tight-knit community that felt more like a production company than a program of study."

Emilygrace Piel, Laramie County Community College and University of Wyoming

REPUTATION AND ALUMNI

So what exactly makes a reputation? Alumni.

Many young people want to start their education at an institution that has a history of sending alumni into the world of commercial success. If NYU Tisch School of the Arts is a catalyst for talents like Whoopi Goldberg, Andy Samberg and Danai Gurira then surely some credit has to go to the department that helped shape and mold them, right? There must be a formula to how the team at Carnegie Mellon School of Drama can get folks like Leslie Odom Jr. and Cherry Jones onto the list of Tony Award-winners, right?

Depending on how you define success and what your aspirations are, you should look into a school's reputation. Most students know the universities and programs that are "ranked as the best in the country" by one source or another. It is these types of programs that have built a reputation for preparing and sending their students to Broadway right after school or landing an agent before they've graduated. If this sort of success is your aspiration, reputation may be a huge factor in your decision. I encourage asking advisers and faculty how their alumni have reached critical and commercial success. Is it in-part because the department invites agents and casting directors to showcases? Is it because their faculty have strong connections within the industry?

A strong reputation does not have to be based solely on alumni--it can also be achieved by the strength of the programs it offers. A small school like Linfield University, just outside of Portland, Oregon has gained a reputation by continually achieving regional and national awards at competitive theatre festivals, providing touring theatre experience by performing at regional high schools each year, and taking its students on annual study-abroad theatre programs to places like Greece, Italy, and England.

On the other hand, if your success plan entails using your art form in a different path or capacity, then perhaps a different brand of "reputation" can be more suitable.

Does the program also have a great directing and playwriting reputation? The networking opportunities between programs can be invaluable. Is performing in new works something that excites you? Then perhaps keeping an eye out for great playwriting and directing programs could help.

Similarly, designers and technicians should look for the aforementioned criteria in addition to considering what defines a design/tech program's success. Perhaps it is the successes, honors and awards won by students at competitions like The United States Institute for Theatre Technology (USITT), the Kennedy Center American College Theatre Festival (KCACTF) and others.

"Some of my favorite performers of color graduated from C.M.U. I figured going there would pave me a path parallel to their careers."
L.H. González, Carnegie Mellon University

"I know other universities boast about their student theatre scene, but Michigan's reputation of an entrepreneurial spirit and community support makes the students especially active. There's always an opportunity to learn, to engage, to witness, or to participate. For instance, my senior thesis was supported by three or four grants from departments and offices outside of the School of Music, Theatre and Dance and engaged students from the engineering, liberal arts, music and Chinese language programs. I also received opportunities to direct on the main-stage venues of Ann Arbor, which include 500 to 3,000 seat theaters! Go Blue!"
Gregory Keng Strasser, University of Michigan

COST

Cost is probably the most important component for students and their families. College is expensive and sometimes a theatre degree can be even more costly. Why? Audition fees, travel to campuses to audition, audition coaches, script purchases—all on top of the regular school's application fees. This is where the most extreme risk is taken by students—is the education financially worthwhile? Will you ever pay your loans off? Is this education an investment in your career?

Generally speaking, liberal arts institutions are cheaper than conservatories. Schools that are genuinely interested in you and eager to get you into their programs may offer talent-based or financial-based scholarships. This is particularly true with graduate programs.

What exactly are you buying with your tuition? When thinking about "worth," consider some of the topics we've discussed—location, reputation, faculty, course curriculum and class size. This is what you are buying and investing in. For each of these aspects, where does it fall when ranked from 1-10 in comparison to the cost? (ex. Is the comparatively high cost worth the quality of Faculty? Is the comparatively low cost worth the class size?) These answers are unique to you. What *you* value most is going to be different than what others do.

Don't let scholarships and/or federal loans hinder this judgment. Remember that loans have interest and you'll have to pay them back over your lifetime. Always look for scholarships, grants and crowdfunding opportunities to help with your education. The stark reality is that most students probably have to work (at least part-time) to help support their ability to train at an institution. The more you can find ways to live, eat, and study as cheaply as possible, the less you will have to pay back later.

"Obtaining a well-rounded education without becoming financially burdened was a major consideration when deciding between relatively affordable four-year universities and incredibly expensive

conservatories. While I acknowledge the value of the more comprehensive courses offered by conservatories, my experience as an artist has been profoundly influenced by my participation in the university environment. Surrounded by so many exceptional individuals on their own journeys, I received invaluable insight into the diverse lives of everyday people, without falling too deep into debt."

Stephanie Lemon, Humboldt State University

"My attendance was based entirely on scholarships. My parents wouldn't let me take out student loans so I could only go somewhere I was covered with scholarships. I ended up taking a summer and winter quarter so I could graduate a semester early."

Jillian Barron, Union University

NAVIGATING YOUR ACCEPTANCES

For every program you are considering, rank each criteria from a scale of 1 to 10. At the end of your process, compare the programs.

Example:

SCHOOL OR PROGRAM: *XYZ University*	
Faculty: *7*	Notes: *Although the faculty is small, they are masters of their craft and have connections in the field.*
Course Curriculum: *7*	Notes: *Love that the curriculum allows for taking design courses, in addition to performance.*
Location: *10*	Notes: *Beautiful location, ideal distance from home, close to an airport, lots of housing options.*
Class Size: *5*	Notes: *Around five students accepted every year for my discipline, wish more were admitted for networking and peer-learning purposes.*
Reputation & Alumni: *10*	Notes: *Great reputation—household name. Alumni are constantly finding work. Particularly strong directing program.*
Cost: *2*	Notes: *Very expensive—will need to look into loans. Not many scholarships available.*
Pros:	Notes: *Sheer name of the program. Easy to travel home for breaks and vacations. Grandma Tillie lives nearby.*
Cons:	Notes: *Expensive tuition and audition process. The acceptance rate.*

SCHOOL OR PROGRAM:	
Faculty:	Notes:
Course Curriculum:	Notes:
Location:	Notes:
Class Size:	Notes:
Reputation & Alumni:	Notes:
Cost:	Notes:
Pros:	Notes:
Cons:	Notes:

THE PERFORMER'S AUDITION

The audition process can be vastly different for each program.

Starting with format, many programs require some kind of in-person audition, either at the school or at a different venue. Examples of other venues include thespian festivals held at each state, various unified auditions, or auditions at the International Thespian Festival held each year at the end of June. Some programs do allow video auditions and some programs don't require an audition at all. Some have more components than just the audition. For example, UCLA has a three-tier process consisting of an audition in front of a panel of faculty, a group movement workshop and an interview with a faculty member. Some programs have callbacks held on-campus, giving room to experience the training, faculty and location.

In terms of content, each program also has different requirements from their prospective students. Instructions can be as broad as wanting "five-minutes of your best monologue(s)" or as specific as "one classic (before 1960), one modern, and 16 or 32 bars of music." Each program's required content can usually be found on departmental websites.

Each audition typically has separate fees as well, hence how this process can get real expensive real quick. Audition fees can range from $50-$100 for each school and if they're involved with URTAs (to get into certain graduate schools) or The National Unified Auditions, those convenings have their own registration fees, too. While it may feel safer to apply and audition for as many programs as you can, consider the overall costs that can accumulate before making this decision.

Some programs utilize audition convening organizations like URTA and The National Unified Auditions. These organizations host bulk auditions and interviews in a single city, throughout a couple days. The biggest perk of this opportunity is not needing to travel to multiple states or counties to audition for schools from around the country and abroad. Other perks include meeting faculty, the ability to ask questions, and the opportunity to receive offers from programs you didn't know existed or schools where you weren't initially auditioning. The UNIFIED auditions and interviews partners with approximately 27 B.F.A. theatre programs, and are held in New York, Chicago and Los Angeles each year. The URTA auditions and interviews represent approximately 45 graduate theatre programs and take place in New York, Chicago and San Francisco each year.

The International Thespian Festival (ITF) auditions and design/tech/management interviews are held each year at the end of June, and starting in 2020 are scheduled to take place at Indiana University where the annual festival now resides. These auditions are seen by 60-75 schools each year. You must be an outgoing junior/incoming senior in high school to audition or share your work at the festival. The hidden cost with the ITF auditions is that you must attend the week-long festival and the cost for room/board/conference fees is about $800.

There are hundreds of theatre audition books and I encourage you to find one (or several) that speaks to you. Also, as you start the audition process, I recommend investing in a reputable acting coach—someone in addition to your high school drama teacher—who has experience crafting monologues for auditions. A good acting coach, combined with a fair amount of preparation, can assist you in finding material, introduce you to key techniques, help you analyze the script and rehearse your pieces until they showcase your best abilities.

"At the in-person audition, I was to perform three pieces: a Shakespeare monologue, a contemporary monologue and a song. After the audition, I was emailed saying I made the final round of auditions which narrowed around 1,000 people to 90. It was then that we were asked to fill out a standard application. After everyone auditioned, they had everyone watch their current show. We were then cycled through four different rooms. Each had a different subject from the curriculum being covered. Overall, it was a pretty rigorous audition process compared to other schools I auditioned with."
Bailey Durnin, Cornish College of the Arts and Pacific Conservatory Theatre

"It was an in-person audition and interview, after an initial audition at a high school theatre festival. The audition and interview were in front of the entire faculty. After auditioning, I received notes and was asked to do it again to make sure that I took direction well."

Veshonte Brown, Troy University

"I did the UNIFIEDs. I auditioned for 22 schools. It was a nerve wracking, stressful, yet exciting experience. I prepared for a year and a half. During my senior year of high school, the process required me to do everything for a 'normal' college application plus auditioning by sending in pre-filmed videos or auditioning in-person."

Emily Sturgess, The Conservatory of Theatre Arts at Webster University

DESIGNERS, TECHNICIANS AND MANAGERS' INTERVIEW AND PORTFOLIO REVIEW

For theatre designers, technicians and managers a different process takes place. The most common process, equivalent to a performer's audition, is a portfolio review and/or interview. Most often, this is done at the school you are applying to, but large, unified interviews are often done in each state and by a couple of organizations.

A portfolio is a professional showcase of your approach, process and final product. Specific elements that have commonly been incorporated in portfolios include:

- Inspiration images, quotes, or collages
- A concept statement
- First drafts or renderings
- Detailed plots
- Art class projects
- Images of you working
- Images of your works-in-process
- Swatches, color palettes or material examples
- Final product (archival images)

Some formal portfolio reviews and/or interviews have separate fees. Fees can range from $50-100 for each school and if they're involved with URTAs or UNIFIEDs, those convenings have their own registration fees, too. While it may feel safer to apply and interview for many programs, consider the overall costs that can accumulate prior to making this decision.

Some programs utilize convening organizations such as URTAs and UNIFIEDs. In addition to serving performers, these organizations host bulk portfolio reviews and interviews in a single city, throughout a couple days. The biggest perk of this opportunity is not needing to travel to multiple states or counties to audition for schools from around the country and abroad. Other perks include being able to meet faculty face-to-face, ask specific questions and get immediate answers and have the opportunity to receive offers from programs you didn't know existed. The UNIFIEDs interviews partners with approximately 27 B.F.A. Theatre programs from around the country, and takes place in New York, Chicago and Los Angeles each year. The URTA auditions and interviews service approximately 45 graduate theatre programs, and take place annually in New York, Chicago and San Francisco.

The International Thespian Festival (ITF) design/tech/management interviews are held each year at the end of June, and starting in 2020 were scheduled to take place at Indiana University where the annual festival now resides. These auditions are seen by 60-75 schools each year. You have to be an outgoing junior/incoming senior in high school to interview and show your work at the festival. The hidden cost with the ITF auditions is that you must attend the week-long festival and the cost for room/board/conference fees is about $800.

These interviews are done in a speed-dating format where each student sits at a table with their portfolio, and the college representatives get two-minutes with each student to see their work and ask questions, then must move to see the next student's work. Several hundred students attend these interviews. It can be a long and tiring process for both the students and the college representatives, but it is definitely worth it.

"I filled out the general admittance application and got accepted. Then I had to do an in-person interview/audition with two bodies of my work about two months after I was accepted."
                                                      Sofia Suro, University of Central Florida

"I went to UNIFIEDs in Los Angeles and had an interview with faculty, showed them my portfolio. They actually kind of glanced over my portfolio and focused more on the interview. The questions weren't as theater-heavy as I thought, they focused a lot on my personality and my wit."
                                                      Shahzad Khan, Carnegie Mellon School of Drama

"I did an in-person portfolio review and interview at the college. While extremely intimidating, this was a very informative process. First of all, interviewing in-person not only gives you the ability to present your entire self, it also gives you the ability to really discover what they are looking for and what the professors are like. As a bonus to doing this at the school they may even give you a more in-depth tour of their spaces and programs that you might not get doing it over the phone or at UNIFIEDs."

Owen Meadows, Emerson College

"My school has open enrollment, but I had to apply separately for the B.F.A. program. I had to submit a portfolio of my work and then attend an interview with the faculty. I felt the interview was very beneficial for me. It was the first time I had really discussed my work as a stage manager in an educational environment and I was able to get good feedback on it."

Finn Nottingham, Utah Valley University

"My advice to students prepping for an interview? Don't procrastinate. Don't be afraid to email the faculty to ask questions. Always bring extra copies of your portfolio and resume."

Jessica Marr, SUNY Purchase

PARENTAL SUPPORT

Making a career in theatre is challenging. You know this. I know this. And especially, your parents know this. However, after studying theatre, students leave with tangible skills that can be used in many career paths (see "Perks of an Arts Education in the Creative Economy" and "Beyond Undergrad" for specific examples). Asking for support from your immediate or extended family may seem daunting, but there are ways to ask for help that are tangible and people can see the results of their support. Here is a start:

Birthday gifts to ask for:

1. Headshots with a professional photographer (these can double as graduation photos)
2. Scripts and theatre books (see supplemental reading list for options)
3. Audition clothes
4. Sheet music for musical theatre auditions
5. Business cards (Vistaprint)
6. Resumes
7. Application & audition fees
8. Audition coach
9. Summer theatre camp tuition
10. Portfolio materials

Parents and/or guardians play a key role in the lives of young, aspiring practitioners. Commonly perceived as a career choice filled with too much risk, it is not uncommon for parents to be wary about their child's decision.

Based on student interviews, here are three discoveries:

1. The students who had the most endearing support were those whose parents or family were involved in, or highly appreciated, the arts. These students were often privileged to start training at a very young age, taking art classes, acting, dance, music, and voice

lessons often since elementary school. These are parents who were supporting the arts, even before having kids.

2. Some parents aren't able to provide much financial support, but students acknowledge that there are many kinds of "support" a parent can provide for them: emotional, spiritual and physical.

3. Those who had little to no support systems in place had/have a more challenging experience entering this industry.

Emotional support can look like many things, but it is evident when parents have healthy conversations with their kids about the difficulties and challenges that are to come in life, in school and in their theatre careers. Once college starts, emotional support can manifest as phone calls of comfort when homesickness kicks in (as it often does), or phone calls of motivation after the inevitable world of "Nos," or, "You're not right for this part," or, "You don't have the prerequisites to take this class" take place.

Financial support is when parents contribute to plane tickets, tuition, audition fees, gas, rent, private classes and all of the other daily expenses that young students face. This is often an under-appreciated support system but is invaluable as a theatre student.

Physical support is when they drive you to auditions and campus visits and when you literally need someone to sit there while you rehearse. Once college starts, this also manifests as a safe and healthy home environment if and when you visit during breaks.

To have any of these types of support is a privilege and should be embraced and never taken for granted. If you don't have this support, what do you do to obtain their or others' support? This is completely circumstantial. For some, their parents' turning point of support is when they won a notable award or talked with a reputable theatre person who confirms their child's talents and abilities. For some, support may never be possible, but students who I spoke to say they used their parents' lack of support as motivation to "make it."

No matter how much your parents are willing (or able) to support you in this endeavor, theatre is a collaborative art form that is inherently supportive. Always feel empowered to create your own "theatre-family" so you can share encouragement, support and resources with each other. You will find that your professors will help be that support, although sometimes this is coupled with "tough love" to make you stronger.

"My parents are both musicians in the music industry, so they know what it's like to devote yourself to a creative life. They have always supported me in my acting, even if they didn't always understand it. And for that, I'm deeply grateful."
Caitlin Kilgore, University of Southern California

"My parents did not expressly forbid me from majoring in theater, though they weren't very pleased about it either. It did help me though, because I had to fight to do something for the first time in my life. At risk of sounding extremely clichéd, I had to realize and prove to myself that majoring and making a career in theater was worth the whole hullabaloo and yelling at Thanksgiving. Thankfully, it is and I'm certain that it will continue to be."
Kellyann Ye, UC Berkeley

"My mother is the most critical part of my success. She has supported me for 19 years, and she continues to give me advice and constant support. By bringing me to the shows she was working on from a young age, I was able to grow up in the theatre. Without her, I would be nowhere near where I am today, and I probably wouldn't even be attending college much less pursuing something I love."
Alanna Manners, University of Central Oklahoma

ENROLLED

First Year

First impressions hold lots of value and you'll be encountering more 'firsts" than you ever have during this year. Peers, staff, faculty, roommates are all people who you'll be working with for the next few years of your life. These introductions can be tricky, especially the ones with your future theatre-family. How do you introduce yourself? What do you talk about? What's the fine line between sharing, sharing too much and bragging—between hustling and staying humble?

Remember that your peers—no matter what the perception is—are there for the same reasons as you: to learn, to immerse and to enjoy. Who has more experience or talent should not be your primary concern. These are the folks with the same industry interests as you and, together, you're the next generation of theatre artists. In an industry where relationships will make or break a career, and word of mouth travels faster than anything else, use common sense. As cliché as it sounds, treat everyone you encounter with the utmost respect. It goes a long way and, chances are, you'll run into them again at some point in your career—and you don't want them to remember you as that rude or obnoxious person.

If you're assigned a faculty adviser, make sure to establish a relationship with them. They can be a great ally throughout your training and beyond. Take advantage of their wealth of knowledge, both of the school and of the industry. It is especially important to privilege your time with them, show up on time, be prepared and be willing to be vulnerable.

Be sure to have a clear understanding of your course trajectory and what classes or units you'll be taking each year in order to finish your degree on time. If you're in a liberal arts institution and pondering the thought of a double-major or a minor, now is a good time to ask how much time this would add to your education plan. If you do decide on a double-major, or a minor, make sure you procure an adviser in your other field of study, too. Often, your advisers can work out difficult scheduling plans together, often making course substitutions if necessary.

Take the first couple of months to acclimate to this new lifestyle and then reflect. If you have time, energy and freedom to get a part-time job, make sure to not cut into the time needed to pass your courses. Flexible jobs are the most ideal as you'll likely find yourself booked mornings for classes and evenings for rehearsals. Some students recommend looking into online or hybrid classes if your institution offers them. These types of classes allow you to do the work at hours that are convenient to you, provide digital lectures and still provide opportunities to meet with instructors during their office hours.

Extracurricular Activities, Clubs and Community Theatre

Most institutions offer an abundance of on-campus extracurricular activities, clubs and communities. Plus, depending on your location, there's a surplus of them off campus: community theatres, regional theatres, speak-easies, etc. Your first and second year at an institution is the ideal time to become acquainted with the ones that spark your interest. Most clubs are low-risk and can provide an excellent opportunity to pick up a new trade, help hone a skill and meet new people. Be open and try something new.

Community theaters are just about everywhere and are frequently seeking fresh talent. While auditioning and participating in outside productions can be beneficial, remember that your priority focus should be the education and training where you're enrolled. Set a limit for yourself based on your circumstances. For example, only commit to doing one show off-campus each year if you are being challenged with on-campus opportunities.

Second/Third Year

Now that you've been introduced to the ins and outs of your school and program, your second and third year serve as a great opportunity to push yourself. Take full advantage of the relationships you've built and the classes you're taking.

Check in with yourself and ask:

- Am I comfortable?
- Am I learning?
- Am I artistically challenging myself?
- Am I taking risks?
- What are my goals for this month and this year?

During your second and third-year, you should begin to get involved with national organizations such as the United States Institute for Theatre and Technology (USITT), the Kennedy Center American College Theatre Festival (KCACTF) and others. These organizations have yearly festivals (in the case of KCACTF they have regional festivals that allow people to qualify for the national festival) that allow students to take a ton of workshops, showcase their work, compete for scholarships and summer employment opportunities and network with other students and industry professionals. Take advantage of these opportunities. Some are slightly expensive (USITT conference in particular), but are definitely worth the investment.

Throughout this time, you should continuously update your resume with all the new shows you've done, mentors you've studied under and new skills you're learning. You may also start looking into designing and building a website for yourself as they are great marketing tools for future opportunities. Some students also start to make a reel for their websites, create professional social media accounts and develop a thorough electronic portfolio in this time.

If you have the privilege of having no commitments over the summer, you may also look into other supplementary summer training programs. These programs will allow you to find a niche you're passionate about, build your resume and continue to grow your network. If this is not an option for you due to financial circumstances, perhaps looking into summer theatre gigs is a more sustainable route.

Some helpful resources to find summer employment include:

- www.backstage.com
- ArtSearch
- Next Step or InterAct (at KCACTF Regional Festivals)
- Joining a Union
- www.lort.org/work

Junior year, you will also want to start considering what life beyond higher education looks like for you. Start a dialogue with your mentors and peers on this topic. How can they help you succeed?

Final Year

Do not lose momentum, continue to grow!

While it can be very easy to get distracted this year, do not quit taking advantage of the advanced courses you're in. During this final year, you should start solidifying what your next steps after graduation are and preparing for this next venture.

Here is a checklist of items you should be working on or complete during your final year. They will equip you with tools needed for any path you choose.

The Final Year Checklist:
1. Prepare a comprehensive audition package
   a) Including 15 contrasting monologues that are appropriate for roles you can be cast in
   b) Including 15 songs, for musical theatre performers
2. Prepare several copies of a physical portfolio
   a) Make your portfolio available digitally, which features at least five of your productions
3. Have nice quality, updated resumes
4. Update and finalize your website (and include on all other print materials)

5. Order high-quality business cards
6. Finish editing your acting reel
7. Have read all of the supplemental reading list that are appropriate for your area of concentration
8. Solicit at least four letters of recommendation from faculty or theatre professionals that are general enough to use for any opportunity
9. Have a list of 10 references, complete with addresses, phone numbers, titles and emails (update every year)
10. Have several audition/interview outfits

Beyond Undergrad

After completing your training, many options lie ahead and, just like the theme of this book, there is no universal "right" choice.

Some of the most common routes graduates have taken are:
- Taking a gap year
- Applying/auditioning for graduate programs
- Finding an agent
- Joining a union
- Freelancing
- Getting a "day job"

The number of routes really are endless, but how exactly do you decide on what is right for you? This is largely a decision made by your gut-instinct, your financial stability and your career goals.

The clearest career paths are those which align with your area of study, for example: actor, costume designer, director, producer, scenic designer, stage manager, etc. However, there are a number of careers that also put your degree to work, as noted below. Similarly, looking at graduate schools is a great opportunity to specify a niche of theatre you are passionate about, as noted below.

Graduate School Majors:

- Acting
- Applied Arts
- Art and Public Policy
- Arts Administration
- Arts Entrepreneurship
- Choreography
- Classical Singing
- Communication
- Contemporary Performance
- Costume Design and Technology
- Dance
- Devised Performance
- Directing
- Dramatic Criticism
- Dramaturgy
- Ensemble-Based Physical Theatre
- European Devised Performance Practice
- Film
- Interactive Media for Performance
- Interdisciplinary Theatre Studies
- Lighting Design
- Musical Composition
- Musical Theatre
- Opera
- Performance Studies
- Performance and Pedagogy
- Playwriting
- Physical Theatre
- Producing
- Production Management
- Scenic Design
- Scenography
- Shakespeare Studies
- Songwriting
- Sound Design
- Stage Management
- Technical Direction
- Television Entertainment
- Theatre Education
- Theatre For Young Audiences
- Theatre History
- Theatre Literature
- Theatre Management

(Alternative) Careers and Industries:

- Amusement Parks
- Artist's Agent
- Artistic Director
- Arts Council Specialist
- Audiobooks
- Broadcast Journalism
- Board Operator
- Booking Agent
- Camp Director / Owner
- Carpenter
- Casinos
- Clown
- Comedian
- Company Manager
- Corporate Trainer
- Creative Team Manager
- Cruise Ships
- Development Director
- Drama Therapist
- Educator
- Electrician
- Entertainment Business Management
- Entrepreneur
- Events Coordinator
- Franchise Design
- Front of House Manager
- Game Design
- General Manager
- Graphic Design
- Grant Writer
- Interior Designer
- Managing Director
- Marketing Director
- Museums
- Outreach Coordinator
- Personal Manager
- Publicist
- Radio
- Real Estate
- Role-Player (for lawyers, medical professionals and government agencies)
- Salesperson
- Sport Mascot
- Stylist
- Theatre Teacher
- Theatre Professor
- Tour Guide
- Videographer
- Wedding Planner
- Window Dresser
- Zoos & Aquariums

ROMAN'S RECOMMENDATIONS

1. Power of Adapting

This first piece of advice was taught to me by a mentor who has had great successes in fundraising, producing, directing and teaching.

The dictionary definition of adaptability is the quality of being able to adjust to new conditions and the capacity to be modified for a new use or purpose. This quality is essential in the success of a young practitioner.

The easiest example of adapting is how to "read a room." Any time you walk into a room—whether for an audition or for an interview—you should already have an idea of who is in there. If you know the department chair is going to be in the room (and this can apply to anyone), this gives you ground to do a bit of research or social media sleuthing:

> What is their background?
> What do you have in common?
> What do they like or not like?
> What shows have they worked on recently?
> What is their sense of humor?

If you can strike a conversation or connection based on one of these questions, it will help distinguish you from others. For example, if I found on social media that I have a mutual friend with one of my interviewers, I will most definitely bring that up to establish conversation. Even a simple Google or LinkedIn search of their name can help you find the places they've lived and worked, which can be used to strike a friendly conversation.

What I mean by "read a room." Adapt to the mood, tone and energy of a room (and the personalities in it), and use that to your advantage. For example, if you have the last audition of the day and the evaluators in the room look tired, you might directly reference this via a joke or by acknowledging their time.

2. Three Circles of Networking

Throughout your life in the theatre, you will hear the word "networking" thrown out a lot. For example, "Going to this workshop is a great networking opportunity" or "I have a great network in Chicago."

Networking generally consists of small talk, learning about another's projects and exchanging of contact information. In my experience, all contacts can be aligned with Three Circles of Networks which are: Influential, Potential Collaborators, and Supporters.

Influential Networks consist of mentors, people in the industry who can get you work, and anyone with a large following - politicians, critics, social media moguls, chefs, or other influencers.

Potential Collaborator Networks are made up of other artists or peers, folks with skill-based resources, and those with physical resources. Examples of skill-based resources include graphic designer, lawyer, intimacy choreography, stitcher. Examples of someone with physical resources include: restaurant owner, print shop owner, or someone with access to rehearsal spaces, etc.

Supporter Networks are comprised of funders, patrons and general followers. Patrons are those who are ticket buyers or who donate to the arts. General followers are those who follow you on social media and anyone you meet who is capable of becoming a patron.

It is important to be able to identify these different networks as every artist employs different marketing, fundraising, and outreach strategies to each one. When I ask for project funding, my Influential Networks receive hand-signed and personalized requests whereas my Supporter Networks will be notified by a Social Media post or mass email. The exact opposite applies when I'm publicizing for a show I've directed: My Influential Networks likely will not come to the show so they receive a standard invite whereas my Supporter Networks are receiving personalized direct messages on social media or personal text messages.

I keep my lists of networks separate and note the folks who fall into more than one category, so I don't reach out to them twice for one project. I also utilize the features on my phone by putting different emojis next to their name that represent something. For example, when I search for "Sacramento" followed by the theatre emoji, all of my previously noted Sacramento-based theatre practitioners will show up in the matches field.

Identify your networks and stay in touch with them. A simple check-in like "How have you been?" or "What are you working on right now?" every couple months will keep you updated with their careers and keep you on their mind.

REFLECTIONS ON EDUCATION

"No single education can fully prepare you for when you get out there. There are always going to be things that we were never taught. However, my education did provide me with confidence in myself as an artist and as a human being. This is the most valuable resource I have received because I feel ready to face the challenges life throws at me with courage and the strength to persevere."

Tyler Szarabajka, Illinois State University

"I feel very confident. My experiences at Boise State University's shows and at regional theatre festivals have been great at filling the gaps in my theater education; gaps that are present because I did not major in theatre."

Celine Meloche, Boise State University

"For an undergrad degree, I feel as though I learned everything I could from the program I was in. The area I feel I'm lacking is the technical/financial part of being an actor. I know next to nothing about equity and agents. What my education did do, though, was strengthen my passion and give me the confidence to pursue that information."

Kellie Wambold, University of Wisconsin at Oshkosh

"I feel confident that I have a toolbox filled with experiences, knowledge and skills that will continue to be filled up as I move along in life. The way that I think about it, learning doesn't stop when you graduate school or finish a class, you should constantly be learning."

Alex Jean, Golden West College and Ithaca College

"I feel tremendously well-prepared. The liberal-arts approach to theater studies is, in my opinion, the best way to prepare for making theater in the real world. There is literally no job I cannot do, which makes me extremely marketable."

Claire F. Martin, University of Puget Sound

GENERAL ADVICE

"Take your time, theatre is not going anywhere. Establish and maintain personal boundaries that work for you, and never be ashamed of having them."
Rebekah Fegan, CSU Sacramento and U.C. San Diego

"Be a part of something you're passionate about. There's so much you can do with an education in theatre, the interpersonal skills are invaluable. If you find yourself going down a path that doesn't feel quite right, switch it up and try a new discipline. Be open to new paths."
Hannah Jane Curry, Linfield University

"You don't have to do something remarkable every day. Growth takes time and is unique to you. Do not judge yourself based on what other people around you are doing. If you are truly passionate about this field, continue to work hard and you will learn crucial skills that will take you into the future."
Alex Tolle, McDaniel College

"Make your own work if you aren't finding it. Sometimes you'll make something that is god awful and that's so okay."
Nathaniel Whitehead, University of Northern Colorado

"Don't get too attached to your designs. You can work on something for weeks only to have the director say 'I hate that'. Communicate early and often."
Tori Storm Buie, University of Arkansas at Fort Smith

"Treat everyone you meet as a potential connection and understand that you are always networking. Continually work hard, even when it seems that little to no progress is, being made and have confidence in yourself even if others don't."
Isabella O'Keeffe, College of the Sequoias

50 THINGS YOU SHOULD KNOW BEFORE YOU START YOUR PROGRAM

1. **Acceptd:** A platform used to apply to visual and performing arts schools, scholarships, festivals and competitions.
2. **Actors Equity Association (AEA):** A labor union representing American Actors and Stage Managers in the theatre.
3. **Agent (Talent or Booking Agent):** Someone who finds and coordinates auditions and jobs for actors, directors, playwrights and other theatre practitioners.
4. **American Theatre Magazine:** The national magazine for the American Theatre. Provides news, features, artist interviews and editorials about theatre in the U.S. and abroad.
5. **ArtSearch:** Produced by Theatre Communications Group, an online theatrical employment bulletin for professionals looking for careers and gigs in the arts.
6. **Blocking:** The precise staging of performers in a show.
7. **Concept Statement:** A short statement that communicates your design ideas for a play to the director and other collaborators so that design unity can be achieved.
8. **Cover Letter:** Typically accompanying a resumé, they provide additional information on your relevant skills and experience for a specific opportunity.
9. **Conservatory:** A college for the study of arts.
10. **Devising:** A method of theatre-making where the "script" is created from collaborative and often improvisational work by an ensemble of performers.
11. **Dramatics Magazine:** High school drama magazine, produced by Educational Theatre Association (EdTA).
12. **Dramaturg:** A dramaturg is a literary editor or adviser who researches, interprets and selects scripts while often doing public relations work.
13. **EDIA:** An acronym for Equity, Diversity, Inclusion and Accessibility. Many iterations of this acronym are used throughout the industry.

14. **Free Application for Federal Student Aid (FAFSA):** A form completed by current and prospective college students to determine their eligibility for student financial aid.
15. **G.E. Courses:** General education classes are the required courses at an academic institution - in arts, humanities, sciences, social sciences and natural sciences.
16. **Google Suite & Gmail:** Google Suite is a variety of applications associated with a Google account including Drive, Classroom, Maps, Docs and Calendar. Gmail is a free email system commonly used in schools and work environments.
17. **Headshot:** A headshot is a portrait where the focus is placed on the person.
18. **International Alliance of Theatrical Stage Employees (IATSE):** A labor union representing technicians, artisans and craftspersons in the entertainment industry including live theatre, motion picture and television production as well as trade shows.
19. **International Thespian Society (ITS):** A division of the Educational Theatre Association, ITS is an honor society for high school and middle school theatre students.
20. **Kennedy Center American College Theatre Festival (KCACTF):** A division of the Kennedy Center, KCACTF is a national theatre program dedicated to the improvement of collegiate theatre in the U.S.
21. **Liberal Arts:** Academic subjects such as literature, philosophy, mathematics and social and physical sciences as distinct from professional and technical subjects.
22. **LinkedIn:** An employment-based social media platform used for professional networking.
23. **Major:** A specific field of study that has mandatory courses or units to fulfill the degree.
24. **Minor:** A specific field of study that has a smaller amount of mandatory courses or units to fulfill the degree.
25. **"Method Acting":** The acting technique in which an actor tries to have a complete emotional connection with a character. Originally based on Stanislavsky's work, the term was coined in the U.S. in the 1930s through the work of the Actors' Studio and Lee Strasberg and Elia Kazan, among others.
26. **Monologue:** A long speech by one actor in a play or movie.

27. **New Play Exchange:** An online script database, search engine and network for playwrights.
28. **Pedagogy:** A method, practice and philosophy behind teaching.
29. **Performer Stuff:** A website, brand and resource for performers to find audition material and noteworthy articles.
30. **Personal Statement:** A very brief written description that highlights what is unique and important to you (can include interests and achievements) and is typically used on applications to educational programs.
31. **Playwright vs Playwriting:** The playwright (spelled this way) is the person that uses playwriting (spelled this way) techniques to create a play.
32. **Portfolio:** A format in which designers and technicians showcase their work.
33. **Publishers:** Most popular script and score publishers include: Concord Theatricals, Dramatists Play Service Inc., Dramatics Play Service, Music Theatre International and Samuel French.
34. **Reel:** A compilation of your work that showcases range for producers, agents and casting directors.
35. **Resumé:** A document used to present their background, skills and accomplishments.
36. **Royalties:** A payment made by one party to another that owns a particular asset.
37. **Screen Actors Guild-American Federation of Television and Radio Artists (SAG-AFTRA):** A labor union representing approximately 160,000 film and television actors, journalists, radio personalities, recurring artists, singers, voice actors and other media professionals.
38. **Scholarships:** A grant or payment made to support a student's education, awarded based on academic or other achievement.
39. **Soliloquy:** A monologue of speaking one's thoughts aloud when by oneself or regardless of any hearers.
40. **Stanislavsky:** A Russian theatre actor and director who founded the Moscow Art Theatre.
41. **Theatre-Schools.Com:** A website that houses lists of all theatre and drama schools in the United States.
42. **"The Canon":** Shows or texts every practitioner should read, according to the mass or popular public.

43. **U-Haul:** A moving equipment and storage rental company. Trust me, save their number.
44. **National Unified Auditions (UNIFIEDS):** Auditions that allow students to audition for numerous university programs in one location over the course of a few days.
45. **United States Institute for Theatre Technology (USITT):** A membership organization which aims to advance the skills and knowledge of theatre, entertainment and performing arts professional involved in the areas of design, production and technology.
46. **Vistaprint**: Resource for business card and other marketing materials' design and production.
47. **W-2, W-4, W-9:** IRS tax forms used to report wages, taxes withheld, etc.
48. **www.wix.com**: A free website design and building platform.
49. **www.wordpress.com**: A free website design and building platform.
50. **YoungArts**: A foundation and program, based in Miami, that identifies the most accomplished high school artists and provides them with creative and professional development opportunities throughout their careers.

SUPPLEMENTAL READING BY CATEGORY

ACTING TECHNIQUE
Being & Doing by Eric Morris
Respect for Acting by Uta Hagen
The Stanislavsky System by Sonia Moore
Improvisation for the Actor by Viola Spolin
How to Speak Shakespeare by Cal Pritner & Louis Colaianni

ADVICE
Letters to a Young Artist by Anna Deavere Smith
The Actor's Life: A Survival Guide by Jenna Fischer
The Artist as Citizen by Joseph W. Polisi
The Dramatic Imagination by Robert Edmond Jones

COLLEGE AUDITIONS
The College Audition: A Guide for High School Students a Degree in Theatre by Tim Evanicki
Before I Got In!: Young Teen's College Audition Guide for Acting and Musical Theatre by Mary Anna Dennard
Before the College Audition by Chelsea Diehl

DIRECTING
A Sense of Direction by William Ball
Notes on Directing by Frank Hauser & Russell Reich
Play Directing by Francis Hodge
The Director's Companion by Mel Shapiro

DESIGN & TECHNICAL THEATRE
Backstage Handbook by Paul Carter
Collaboration in Theatre by Rob Roznoski & Kirk Domer
Scene Design and Stage Lighting by Parker, Wolf, & Block
Theatre Design & Technology Workbook by Derek R. Lane
The Costume Technician's Handbook by Rosemary Ingham and Liz Covey
Sound and Music for the Theatre by Deena Kaye and James LeBrecht

MANAGEMENT
Creating Great Visitor Experiences by Stephanie Weaver
Management and the Arts by William J. Byrnes
The Backstage Guide to Stage Management by Thomas Kelly
The Stage Management Handbook by Daniel A. Ionazzi

SCRIPTS (MODERN: 1950-2000)
A Raisin in the Sun by Lorraine Hansberry
A Streetcar Named Desire by Tennessee Williams
Angels in America by Tony Kushner
August Wilson's 10 Plays aka *The Pittsburgh Cycle*
How I Learned to Drive by Paula Vogel
Night, Mother by Marsha Norman
Noises Off by Michael Frayn
Rhinoceros by Eugene Ionesco
The Crucible by Arthur Miller
The Odd Couple (Female Version) by Neil Simon
The Vagina Monologues by Eve Ensler
True West by Sam Shepard
Zoot Suit by Luis Valdez

SCRIPTS (CONTEMPORARY: 2001-Present)
August: Osage County by Tracy Letts
Clybourne Park by Bruce Norris
Doubt: A Parable by John Patrick Shanley
God of Carnage by Yasmina Reza
In The Next Room or *The Vibrator Play* by Sarah Ruhl
Indecent by Paula Vogel
Red by John Logan
Slave Play by Jeremy O. Harris
Speech & Debate by Stephen Karam
Sweat by Lynn Nottage
The Laramie Project by Moisés Kaufman and Stephen Belber
The Wolves by Sarah DeLappe
Topdog/Underdog by Suzan-Lori Parks

SPECIAL THANKS

A tremendous and profound thank you to all of the people below, and to the hundreds not in the book who shared their time, stories and reflections with me. Truly, without them, this book would not be possible.

Susan Abbey, *Brigham Young University, M.F.A.*
Hunter Anderson, *Hastings College*
Belle Aykroyd, *American Conservatory Theater, M.F.A.*
Jillian Barron, *Union University*
Veshonte Brown, *Troy University*
Tori Storm Buie, *University of Arkansas at Fort Smith*
Miranda Erin Campbell, *Purdue University*
Martin William Cicco Jr., *University of South Alabama*
Hannah Cohen, *New York University*
Heather E. Cribbs, *Flagler College*
Hannah Jane Curry, *Linfield University*
Bailey Durnin, *Cornish College of the Arts; Pacific Conservatory Theatre*
Tyler Joseph Ellis, *University of Southern California*
Rebekah Fegan, *CSU Sacramento; UC San Diego, M.F.A.*
Michael Fields, *University of San Francisco*
Meghann Heinrich, *Walla Walla University*
Brenda Hubbard, *Ohio University; University of Washington; University of Portland, M.F.A.*
Kelsey N. Forero, *Valencia College; North Carolina School of the Arts*
L.H. González, *Carnegie Mellon School of Drama*
Carson Harvey, *SUNY Purchase*
Jennifer Horne, *The American Musical and Dramatic Academy*
Kiara Hudlin, *Humboldt State University*
Alex Jean, *Golden West College; Ithaca College*
Antoine Johnson Jr., *Linfield University*
Haley Johnson, *Graceland University*
Shahzad Khan, *Carnegie Mellon School of Drama*
Caitlin Kilgore, *University of Southern California*
Shea King, *Humboldt State University; University of Idaho, M.F.A.*
Derek Lane, *Seattle Pacific University; Western Oregon University, M.A.T.; San Diego State University, M.F.A. & M.A.*
Stephanie Lemon, *Humboldt State University*

Alanna Manners, *University of Central Oklahoma*
Maggie Markham, *Boston University*
Justine Marler, *University of North Carolina School of the Arts*
Jessica Marr, *SUNY Purchase*
Claire F. Martin, *University of Puget Sound*
Caitlin McFann, *San Francisco State University*
Owen Meadows, *Emerson College*
Hannah Muren, *The Conservatory of Theatre Arts at Webster University*
Finn Nottingham, *Utah Valley University*
Isabella O'Keeffe, *College of the Sequoias*
Emilygrace Piel, *Laramie County Community College; University of Wyoming*
Antonio Romero Jr., *The University of Texas at El Paso*
Lynne Marie Rosenberg, *Vassar College*
Celine Meloche, *Boise State University*
Rae Robison, *Missouri Valley College; UC Irvine, M.F.A.*
Kaitlyn Samuel Rosin, *University of Evansville; Actors Studio Drama School, M.F.A.*
Raymond Scholl II, *New Hampshire Community College*
Melissa Schwarz, *CSU Northridge*
CamRon Stewart, *University of North Carolina School of the Arts*
Gregory Keng Strasser, *University of Michigan at Ann Arbor*
Jo Strom Lane, *University of Arizona; Central Washington University, MA; University of Connecticut*
Emily Sturgess, *The Conservatory of Theatre Arts at Webster University*
Sofia Suro, *University of Central Florida*
Tyler Szarabajka, *Illinois State University*
Alex Tolle, *McDaniel College*
Epigmenio Villareal, *Taylor University*
Caitlin Volz, *Chapman University; Yale School of Drama, M.F.A.*
Kellie Wambold, *University of Wisconsin at Oshkosh*
Nathaniel Whitehead, *University of Northern Colorado*
Kellyann Ye, *University of California at Berkeley*

ABOUT ROMAN SANCHEZ

Roman Sanchez currently serves as an associate governmental program analyst for the California Arts Council, founding artistic director of Lime Arts Productions and was recently the assistant executive director and a resident artist at Dell'Arte International. He is a Kennedy Center National Arts Impact Award recipient, Herb Alpert Theatre Scholarship recipient and was one of American Theatre's "Six Theatre Practitioners You Should Know." He's served on boards of various art nonprofits—contributing to education, development and programming initiatives.

Under Roman's tutelage as an acting coach, students have gone on to win local and regional competitions, gain acceptance into their dream undergraduate and graduate schools, and land gigs around the country. In particular, he is well-known for his master classes in Artist Branding, EDIA (Equity, Diversity, Inclusion & Accessibility) in Theatre, Peer Pressure: Working With Your Peers, Theatre Beyond High School: The Next Steps, and Young Entrepreneurship: Getting What You Want.

He trained at Central Washington University, Humboldt State University, The Artist as Citizen Conference at The Juilliard School, Stagecraft Institute of Las Vegas and The Kennedy Center.

Oh, and he's 22 years old.